Sarah Riggs

Lines

Winter Editions, 2025

Lines

for Lyn Hejinian

I'm interested in the ludic aspects of language and literature, the idea of playing a game with rules that can be broken. For me it was important to break the rules in a selective or systematic way . . .

Aimé Césaire had a way of making fun of the language of power in his work, and he was conscious of how Caribbean and African people altered the languages of European colonizers.

—Harryette Mullen, *Looking Up Harryette Mullen: Interviews on* Sleeping with the Dictionary *and Other Works* by Barbara Henning

I am always conscious of the disquieting runs of life slipping by, that the message remains undelivered, opposed to me . . .

It is impossible to carry light and darkness, proximity, chance, movement, restlessness, and thought. From all of these, something spills . . .

—Lyn Hejinian, *Writing Is an Aid to Memory*

I had an idea to write a book that would translate the detail of thought from a day to language like a dream transformed to read as it does, everything, a book that would end before it started in time to prove the day like the dream has everything in it, to do this without remembering like a dream inciting writing continuously for as long as you stand up till you fall down like in a story to show and possess everything we know because having it all at once is performing a magical service for survival by the use of the mind like memory.

—Bernadette Mayer, *Midwinter Day*

October 15, 2018

You had a dozen up your sleeve anyway

Possibly lozenges, some sort of sucking

The freeze and the heat: living with extremes

Merely to tell the tale over and over

Such was the answer in a place of no answers

We could collect the ties and ropes

Turning on hollows and mounds: frightened

Along the tying of knots some sentiment

How to tell you this query

When you were rustling in the drawer

And a listening settling into the turtles

We had heard the prayers of tigers

Mock eagles soaring over garbage dumps

Paused and reaching for a hand

On each side some talk of it

How to tell at the last moorings

Sensational speech rivered into whisper

Beings test for ground at sparkle

Remain days at an oar pull and repeat

Yes to the lick of that spoon once

Up, up, up the river surely

A pitch of it, into the glove without body

Take turns at recalling further

Much to the axe of it, at toothpick

Announce the flavors as cherry, rhubarb, and hazelnut

And if you could see things they can't

The numbers of days reel like in a slot machine

Who could tell you any more or better

October 16

The who of the forsworn is apple

Dominion peaks and a range of eyelashes

Frontal some quick remarks and a landing

More to the memory in a seat back there

Querulous along a range of hearts

Six to the pupils in the row left of center

Dimension zero they had had enough

Or else it was an answering machine

Over time some tarts and fruit remainders

To that oven where she deigned to lay her head

Approximately questioned furthermore

Any apple was dandy so say the quick

Had it concerned you well then merry

Sometime rafters as place holders

Barking along a grin of fur

We determined that it be laid down

Here along a ground of holes

She had said to the rafters: a trumpet song

And it was keen, that edge, in a major key

Swiftly removed and contorted into that image of a bus

Silently deprived of now grins

Making some kind of backyard music

It is arranged just so and so

Or a quiver, multi-dimensional, in the breast

I wake to alternate intake, at an angle

She thought it more or less certain (they did, they)

How quickly the rumpus begins

To know no beginning to endings

Me was I sleeping or just alive

Frontally along a rip tide

They vouchsafed an arrival

Too many meters down, kindred spirit

To the alert gains, troubled soul

Merely this matter, once again, again

Your life a line along which you coast

Some catch fevers and zing

Thoroughly braided, a kind of victory

Throw it to the moon you say, and I listen

Making way through fires & floods

The past rejoins us and we are here

Sinking in all that cannot be changed fast enough

October 17

It was a twirl into a tweet into land

You were sorry for the lane

Frightening mere reminders of curl

The excuse was ever plain and recorded

We admired the delicacy of it

And calling back to the first row

Meretricious that was so

Some statements made without proof

And this changes things

How to admire and appreciate simply

Concluding this hour is a loss

They had surrendered our conviction

Merely judgmental and kind

It was infectious taking off layers

To be honest, a turn in time

Not to be kidding with you

How restless and uncertain

Frilly the midst of telling

Jumping back onto mere conviction

Lazy too and some animals

We couldn't be bothered

Aware of the resonance back there

What it would take to flip the world

A coin of sorts, no this fate instead

All the mini-decisions made differently

Unimaginable, hard to believe

Query into mass ache

The fierceness of the drive to destroy

From a mass of glimmering

We too could not sunder

Degrees of hatred technically

Floating back amid the din

Surely something to say or do

Frosty, quickly back there

And if she falls others will be there to catch her

The terrific measure of listening

Rounding up the time asking it to comply

Letters to the weather, asking it to please stop

When to the bridge of the nose, crossing

Zealous and quite determined there

Mainly deranged, in good company

Rarely hunting for anything else

Masters of disguise, masters of looting

We remembered what you said and had it framed

Wishing it would fly this way

And we would catch it in our ears, and split ground

October 17

Merely a train into reason

Stopping for you and you and them

Memories of a cavern and beam of sunlight

Still a few wished to be colorblind

What was this refusal to see

Always these gestures that remember their pain

No, no, no. That's too many no's for taste

Once let in the door they could walk through the whole hour

Children pour out of your bedrooms and onto the sidewalk

I thought it round and whole

We too agreed on the level of toxicity

Carried away by motion more to the point

Laid out together, fingers next to fingers

Some thought it cruel

Bodies being moved around

Not to relax while this is going on

Carefully to assume a posture of understanding

Returned to the place of place

Marvelously present those eyes

And then a slur and all the work that needs to get done

And the heart of the incident cannot be removed

Some caution while hot

What was tempting removed

Many in a struggle toward breath

Seven-and-forty swans or how many at Coole

And some willingness to change

There were fourteen back there

Making the night an eye opener

Such that talking together: carrots

And if she can't relate

Quickly to say to speak

All ears in the waiting room

Gently that nudge comes

To sit back and breathe

Millions of others just like him

October 22

She to the willow of grass to tell

Four or more and some strains

Mirth in mirror forsake to say

Salient to the pitch maybe sunken

How to tell that time and under time

More remainders and singing to something

Curly into zone match along trying

Others bewildered also these answers

Furthermore to hear, walk into the inner ear

Strange furniture and paprika

More endeared and wandering these ways

A yielding and a foreclosure on rhyme

Sleepy to the Zen burial and rebirth

Frail along lake which indrawn

Some cacophony and cooperation

The telling of said hour, say say

Meek in a mouthing to the second

Mixed in with the artichokes

Some others were candy flowers and hues

Deliberate quicks in the interruption atmosphere

Melody and votes and suggestions

He caw and she forthwith cups

And the milling in the 8-shapes and answers 8

Cryptic but determined with direction

Sold to the woman in the red

A thousand more cued into battle

Hayseed and floss contagion unspread

Quickly upward glow familiar

Then surprising in a quill hers

Frozen remainders of chippers and it

A gull and sturdy telling at the mane

And you and you and me and me

Querulous entries into thankful praise

Subdued and asking, then to let go

No not that or that, no less no's

It was a swirling and become, free to tell

Thought ventures into main and the shortcoming

Had it been there, the intuition?

Yes yes and there not surrendering

Not to let it get swallowed, no, No

October 23

Close to the bone the laws clamp down

Rendering the energy red and an ear purr

Like clockword the mooring into amble

Solutions free of solemnity in improv

Could we take an ounce of attitude

Frozen pathways scramble the soul

And a mere mellowing into ailments

Some examples of anything foretold

Along an angle toward voicing

Dissent and disentanglement, anger

Efforts to comprehend and tell

Quick concurrency shelled meanings

The rhizomatic growth outdated

She to the owl along quixotic wisdom

At the same time, you would say

Kittens flying into the texture

Salt to tongue, talking pretty

Land rights, dimension and quirk

We recalled happily to the left

Generative disposal into lane

Awful the power of the awful

And hinted back denial

Quickly removing rights like bark

Forlorn and yet even comforter

Much amble and ferocity

Programmed to perform removal

Stripping away possibility to speak

An undercurrent of power, fish tails

Remaining motives and succotash

Formidable energy at the outset

The laws tangled in rights

The rights removed, layer after layer

Naked greed and hatred this color

The skin not articulate

Overheard wishes for demands

To let go also a way toward power

Keenly the dimensional vote

Over whom would win, simple as that

Let's take back this place

Under and out the entrances

Multiple sanity asked for

Quixotic murk and some general hair

How to revolt in the morass

Actually what I had to say

Tangled up, in, thrown about

Catch the curve and tale

Lately some too disturbing

October 24

A quick sort of quiver in

Twas truth be told in degrees

Some rainstop hours in wilding

Quaint but determined so be it

Thick in rain also music and time

To remove from the list asking questions

Supposedly to explain in drudgery

Merely windows out such curve

Formerly displaying lodgings

How to remain in speech dwellings

Doors into intimacy (which hasn't always gone so well)

To further the directions

The mainly dependent cloaks

Bruskly pushed aside in peonies

Stalks and output further deranged

Queries into animal queendoms

Fortunately stepping into melodies

Casting a glance or spell or island

Murky communication replaced

Salient questions and apostrophes

Dangling leaves and sentences

From dropped equations brisk

Ask the fortunate

Marked panels in layman's tools

More falls from places unknown

We had rehearsed the table

Forward relegated departure circles

A cask and a place to disappear into earth

For to the rain of it ample

A wisp and three-legged place named

Me and you and you apt and sure

Surely toe after toe we believed

And asked for reprieve you to give

Some moved or texted it wasn't clear

Or danced or wrote in patterns

The entry was in keeping

Just and salty desserts held there

Me also me and we in the risk

Kindly gesturing this way this way this way

Are there wrong ways, do you feel?

Can you calculate the weight in emotions?

Have you a place to go above your liver?

When is the last chance?

May you remember all that gone?

And when will you and I deliver the peace

October 25

Some clear direction in the mist

Had you barreled over rage

There were windows in what you were saying

And we were listening to the rain in your eyes

Assorted thoughts and musings

Gullible but slippery ideas

If we could forgive the avalanche

Or the tossed reprieves to the whole

Merely zoned in quick response

You had the tremor of insight

Not the only one in seeing

Questions right left and under

Myriad dots to that maze leading when

Fortunately crowned ordinary

And there was a missing foot in your thought process

Others deterred by who we became

Tenderly an advantage to the declarative

Must be quick, sharp, darting

There trapped some play how when

Dastardly eager or remiss

Top coats and fur tuxedo ears

Ways toward voting in blue

These jacks and particulars thrown down

If you could reply, press send

More to the side a dimension

Deterred nonetheless formidable

Quirks and bows bending laws

Such fierce clamping around difference

Others decide how to trickle

Lanes of cacophony to the left of right

An indigenous presence hear strong

The leaves crimson with the blood of it

Not yours, taken, scuttled away

The squirrels and the dear embodying the crimes

Every building violent to that ear

The listening, to feel the curve of it

Memories root in pavement

Trajectories maimed for it is a circle

Not to go in that direction

Forward not a place: it is around

And back into the earth place

The words sprout leaves

Come to an understanding

Talk to the wind of it

Hold out some acorns with worms

A music to the air, acceptance of our ends

October 29

Timidly the place names end up

The laugh of the chronic fog inland

Melt into meadows dementia

Some mess of emotions unsorted

Held and released into the undersea

Such quaver in a raw nest

It stretched and curled

There to the gift diluted

Quandary among engagement twist

Thoroughly fierce and top-hatted

Ocean features questioned and deleted

Mixed with rain alongside it

Same to mellow remarking or making

Here a cuff, there a key, which way

Out along tissues of quandary

Minimalist gestures toward reward

Planets doing their unusual rotations

With difference an assured tangle

Makeshift dependence toppled

Underling waiting there panting

Frozen cuffs of diminishment tendered

If you too tremendous along thinking

Wakefulness and mind-tripping

Save space time dimension circling

Data be sure if keen-hearted

Wanderlust to be true to painting it

Bring up the reverence twice over

Disjointed telling cues in lying there

Foretelling foster along Avenue A

More quiet decided replenishment

Zone analysis to the waving

Minority position splitting

Zany scrutiny stretched out

Decided rolls of rejoinders

Salamander toes and some moles

Late stepping ears back there

Query into forlorn maintenance

Fraught lines of thread over heads

Some quicksilver and question marks

To be sure the sails out from under

Forewarnings of temptation

Sickle cells and dime imprints

Wayward candles marking it

Sister into prolonging the attachment

Minuscule blackouts to time

October 30

Then again the ends of land

Twirl amid a deranged crowd

Soporific melodies and quicksilver

Touch the curve of lies

Frozen removal of a keen sense

Migrant thoughts=needs=not later

She heard you back there versing

There were several deliveries of insight

Something tightened the protuberance

Willful sadness absorbing the rain

To pick up and hold in there

A mandate, a duck, two pens

If we repeated it dimensionally

Lick to the flavor of dismissal

Quaint arias inflecting the mood

It erupted from the sides that way

Give answers and gait

The younger hallowed be night

We wished it on you, to imagine

Indulgent sieve, let through meaning

Tenacious in the remarking

To line up in a circle testing it

Quarantined, sudden release, disease

What was the telling, regrouped, foreclosed

Catechism, motley, loss swaying

Actual minutes, you toward the can

If it could be regrouped to the mellow

Dethawing districts, it would take at least that

Dismantled, getting it sorted, jumble

That way, again, but differently

Some kind of mango-flavored rind

Needs along one railroad track

Ripples of grief in the eyelids

Rivers, tides: why we call them

Bodies of water, hurtling about

Hold yourselves, beating hearts

Whether we like it or not, we are together

No answers in the newspapers

Syndrome of those who care too much

November 5, 2018

Some thought it was groundless

Four or more and a cat equals many

Zany the rhythms and returns

Quick to the punch further in there

Calamari and lotion way of making sense

There was madness at the edges of the Guggenheim

Convene with spirits, draw them down

More retreats into bread and butter

Carefully distinguish haunts

The table turned over and the cards

Wishing it otherwise to talk to people

Conversely some souls dragged out of beds

We too too close to the wish bone

And if you murmured response

Straightforward this time ripping

The passages redirected, separated

Furthermore a tremendous lengthening

How to swim that channel

Left to meander among the scraps

Finding it scrappy and a relief

From the taut cube light shades

Other words allowed in & treated melancholically

There was a firm collectivity

Inevitable name-calling into death

Alternate routes not really advised so close to the end

To do nothing for a while: this is radical

Some dimension clearly out

Far-fangled lip service to disgruntle

November 8

The remainder of the calm fleeting

A nexus of determined positions

Conflicting deterrents and toxins

What to the message of lane

Fiercely interacting particles

A cue to tend to the margins

More or less mesmerized by the star dust

For a range of meander to the zones

Quickly drawn in a circle of shades

Fortunately crossed with ambiguity

Damaging spirals and twists

Land-locked fevers and nightmares

Debilitating sadness and reach

More along sensing the November holes

Secondly destitute in so much running water

The momentum from the cases

A crust of silence and know how

Depending on determinacy chairs

Pull up and participate a while

Say to the circle what goes around

Curtailed diagonals and crossbows

Limit the know-how in house

Dangle from the answers' delay

Frightening repercussions and words

What syllables in here we find

After all some dimensions of senility

Candied apples and stuck teeth

Who to the umpteenth hour

Details along a kind telling

You foreclosed the discussion

And a cawing of the absent crows

Merely to glean some sense from it

Depend on withdrawal and taper

Front to side, across and back, around

Tell the tapering objects

Difficulty to articulate the cross-check

Further delays in darkness

Changeovers and frontal queries

Quirks of emotion, call it what you will

Racing by to a general slow-down

Others delight in the crush

Formerly known as content

November 13

Rain beads drop profusely

Some merit test the waters

How were we going to explain

Lest we fall into negativity

You owned up your tears

Further to repeat the kindness

Bent along a torpor

Rush sights and formulas

To contain in there dimension

The main merriment disaster

Tossed inkling of quicksand

The value of betrayal

Heartened in liquidity

Long-matched fortune to call

Lost in it: a pyramid of words

Zany completion hour

The wishlist sharpened

Cues to testing in an apple

It was the big one: all of it is important

At the cusp of madness them there

Looking into the mouth of the volcano

We are assembled, each touching

Like-minded, individuated, together

This to be told, parsed out at the seams

A range of tossed observations

Lately the tests exacting into

Lest we be deranged by time

Unless it is space to be devoured

Curtailed and inward, out out damn

Recourse to spots of time

Furnished and beheld the awe

Felt together what it is we love

If there could be a dent into attestation

Left-minded, something in the brain

Disagree with you, just here

In cue with foretaste

The common call, one bird in one forest

Round the bed of it

Some time for births and renaming

Cast back in remove

Tasks in order of appreciation

Cauter the fellows

X marks the spot still

Things I had to tell you were

Formerly and future cue

November 14

Only hour only thought: speech speech

Tell it juice heft and slant

Warily amuse once again

Some futuricity to say

Other word other anger other other

Between them, a footprint the size of Manhattan

Underscore the elements maybe

A furry designer into deer

Wake into a glancing dream, do I?

Frontier main into malleable

Walk on a planet that melts, moves

Thought to assemble a few continents

How to, the lanes toward disaster

Hard to find a place to step

Speak speak, breasts, what the mouth doesn't know

Five tracks toward a stigmatism

Otherwise a crossing over now's

To the skin hard cross

What were so so so

Quickly into chaos, millions go

The thing I meant to tell you

I am in a constant state of forgetting

How to drum up the collective energy

Can you start hoarsely

Forgiving the moment into second

Deranged colors of rage and other elements

What you sacrifice to tell

A toss-up suddenly revealed

It was a wish understanding

A nerve, hit, truth a what's it

Angle into artery, a coursing wish list

Can you derange or angle

In a positive how many negatives again?

Sails warping into butterfly

A cost made up of soul

If they could agree, the sky

Telling again & again

You, a wish for cathedral, touch

November 15

The assured rise in expectations

Flurry of the soul to fault

More candid in the aftermath

Telling repercussions lest we be

A haunted sort of twangling

Zero carve under: a minus zone

Where to the time of splinter

Agree in space sleet of thought

Thicket of removal whether used tickets

Sure padding along containment

Sixth trajectory at finger wave

A scuttle of myriad individual feelers

Carry the weight of know-how

Frankly abutting loss of minute gestures

So to the wind or trolley, jump on

Going to a scene inside of one

Strength of meander not lost

Eventually to find a response

Torn the tether of intuition

A register of mind temperatures

Callously pick at the center

It cannot hold this widening gyre

Everyone's death on your tongue tip

Prefer laughter to extinction

The least rope around speech

Tway it true, spitious trackle

Trein in fitps washt

Crusp tanglest feep

Tallp ofn qwirp

Frip tway trusilience

Mwart tisper clotps

Shpreverst tumple

Frape quindlsnatch

A froth of quipperwill

Designated framember

Quick to the will of coughing

Mented clucking and zane

Fortuitous further duck

Planned along colors

A zepiter mouth timin

Shuckle and haste to backwards bobbin

Frickle zumious bandersnatch

Zupittle carving blade beyond

Tumble worth twer match

January 1, 2019

The rain had amended it in fossil fuel

And the soul turned back from life

Over there behind the shelf rich rinds

A precious flourish of tangerines

You to the kilometer of smiles

Mainly quickened by the pulse of terrain

Lush solutions to a ceviche arrival

Merely demeanor how to the tongue

Crackling fissures into matcha

Some reason overturning the rest break

Wave repetitions along bees and baby insects

These sick days making themselves known

January 2

Turn upon affirmative x chance

Trained to whale outwards

Tickle the assumptions of Q

Tear at the range of notions

Emotion F torn in at the capital

Some other letters scattered and regrouped

It was what we deliberately hoped

Saturninely wished in the Hiroshige owl

A tear suspended there for a while

Ranged over the suspicious bridge

Rarely catered to the embryo howl

And then furious mossy ways

Q again Q and again remarkable

It would have to be the River House

January 3

For now in a quiet howling

Some rest and recuperation offered

And the night monsters foiled just now

They'd be back and we too, we too

It was in our nature to be split

To want this and this, and this not the same

How ever it was presented, tangled

The twice witches cackling in the air

The scent of grasshopper, a salt of worm

They refused any potion along ways

It was up to the cats two know (we'd ask)

Some thoughts as to where the where-wolves were

Had trickled in the seems & ambivalences

Peculiar washes trained into action

You too along the sides of knowing

Memorable favors discussed at random

The trick to understanding in vain

Tear drops in pen along your notebook

Also offering some steps as up a ship's side

Another dozen facetious options glide by

"I laugh less" said Douglas Dunn

Other quotables lining up

A small stuffed turtle & koala & baby

The stuffing replacing animals historically

Lax members of congress knocking

A general pulsing and shaking

"we used to hide under our desks"

The nuclear threat, what was it now

Now, now, now some surprises in the arrangements

Especially if a ramp is not the thing

Remove please & offer candy instead

Such thoughts occurred in spades

And the queen of hearts was you

Is you and you walk into a room

And you leap for a fortnight

On that net and there is no poetry

You are on the trampoline

Old friendships, yours, your father's rise

A woman who loves us all flies from Colorado

And a gathering at Tuesday noon

Four women and one man

Finding the path to accompany the female ancestors

Where I began

January 8

The assemblage of emotions added up to a solid object

We could buy or not, wrestle or rustle forth

Others lined up to see, and you got in line

Some mistaking it for ornament, rose or shell

The quick of concentration: there

Perhaps like what swirled out of any person

From and with body, and with it, very much so

Animals, even trees

I contradict myself, you won't be able to buy it

And it is not solid anyway

January 13

Languishing moths and a nighttime of grief

Wake, wake to the time, remaindered in

Some removal of haunts & whispers

Challenged in an after hour

They too formally crying this thing

Walking tumultuously along each foot

Scaled back way back some moon time

Other hands in the timed pleas

Yet colluding, decidedly advantaged

More to telling wears a tear along it

We too churning weak four tweets

The thought of you returning wildly

Query mellow into follow

A container frequency delectably

Zone X a place into diving

Formidable land's beginning a swallow

Lest quirk in the frame malleable

Ancient blessings lame to the angle

Further kindness waking into tri-second

Deft traits into wobbly acceptance

Future loss into harrowed dementia

Same lands tried back how to

Lately smiling into bifurcated kindness

Others shrunken solemnly into ink

Quirk X followed by eyebrow Z

Telling repose into an angle back there

Fortunately in layers to be

Foretaste of taboo feast anchoring

They thought in webs of brain matter

How does it all work, precisely?

Two in a bush one in the hand

That's not it worth saying deftly

Curtailed at the impasse of Q without A

A refusal to say, to ask, to care

Many mongering minds developed inward

Way to address a person without address

Merely mentor the mellowed out

Such dexterity in teething as this age

Out of joint the calendar closed in

Sayings stacked into weak piles

And the words wobbling along

Or a methodical yawn in the gap

Patient far from symptom or sunset

This half-moon telling what & how

Lest it be said that there were imperfections

Everyone knew everything anyhow

January 21

The remaining land dwarfed by peculiar tides

Mountains of clocks telling the time backwards

Other arrows hitting the spot of a thousand birds

Mainly sidelined by a gorgeous matter

Some derangement in the quickening ferocity

A cane of support landing in this spot

How to deter the seconds in a question

That too could be terrible affect

A foray or fray thought to be

A million other meanings by that blunt appraisal

Further removal into sidelines sparkling

Many an only one super blood wolf moon

Quickly monitoring the arrival of wings

Other demands upon waters tested

Flurries of souls waving to their bodies

Lifting up the dichotomy and cracking shell and all

Lessons in dementia strange alibis

More arrangements to melodic staying power

Curled and wagging out plaintive beats

Currently an aspen or birch how to distinguish

A boat sinking or running adrift

The telling of trying to get somewhere

Notary republic pained in its sides

Stretch out the damage and sit back

Awful pungent odor of a mind's ailment

Quick to distinguish the winning lottery

Others foregrounded in yay-saying

You could ride quick along a hem

And debris caught in a national holiday

Sweet frost along canine teeth

A remark toward howling

These to the whole whole whole

January 24

A removal of grins into that explosion

Her life different from that point forward

A further circle into wind and direction

Call for relics and a swelling monument

The repeated into winging careers

Brushed into angle X

The quixotic terrain further into Y

Some changed formulas set through

Further along the tides removed

You too tell the waking venue

Other textures and colors in there

Some window arrival seating along

Other menus and selections

She reiterated the collective wishes

It was really telling the analogue of stories

Myriad planes and emotions

A discussion of pallor and trembling

Fingers crossed for a very long stretch

You too formalize the windows

Framed in the alleyways a saying

Hollowed-out nimbus

What does it take to understand

To slow down, let the emotion out

A hard tip of time and held there

A song continuous drifts up

The healing power of these minutes

There was an engraving in there, more than one

February 1, 2019

The thing was the which interpreted out

Whatever feature of extreme analysis

Teeth to the grind the pain absorbed in

Tossed about inside a flame in the wind

Stories in there about how hard it would be

For the other the other the other (not me)

If answering personally for history's wrongs

Some sides cutting at the organs

And if we are one piece, this is of a piece

Challenged to the telling in place

A Rubik's cube inside the stomach

Working it till all the colors come to separate sides

Connected and comfortable

So this is the way you like it?

Apparently the body rebels

Knots and bends, twists and imbalances

Halved in the middle

Like swallowing an iceberg as a child

It won't melt it hides in the body's warmth

The warmth must come from thoughts

They jut about and spin as daggers

The discrimination in the brain

You are not the only one

But you must live to evolve with it

In order to survive mentally

You out yourself here

February 11

A thought crept into the statement

Physical sensations receive knowledge

The query a fellow train tender

They quizzically tendered that way

They had heard of the awful mess

We were prepared to change

It would require something beyond

What we could currently imagine

Further insistence on shifting the half-buried interior

The interiors of great grandparents

Inherited, heavy, as so much furniture

To take this interior furniture and put it

On the outside

So that we would know

To go forward, insist upon that

Some conditions to remove mastery

Others had zoned in on bravura

Some would not be changed

And bias and prejudice are in the genetic material now?

How many souls could unravel to reveal differences?

And what is difference and is there a core?

A tender line of words with inflections of thought

Harbingers of thought, into the cadence

Challenging notions of the interior

What return with change on the keyboard

Some mention of meander

Direct the lines outward with compassion

A mountain of understanding to digest

Other opinions on the subject footers

A reprieve from demand, such eloquence

It was a statement, heard, not said

There along the avenue, treatment

Cues to ear, an operative dimension

Cutaneous saga of lobes

Off to other planets, this to mention it

A choice in rearing what figures

February 21

It was generative and telling

The whisper at the bridge

Several in quick fusion

Taper the sands

Frontal the imagination and a squeeze

To wind at the street

At the mouth, at the front

The issue with saying, tempt

The word relayed an event or question

Some talk in the mouthful, deranged

Back to that degree

And the investment in submerged feelings

All those fears coming to the surface

& being dealt with

People talking about what things felt like

Further along dementia an open conversation?

It was a choice, telling how it was

March 7 & 9, 2019

The bodies in the rafters as metaphors

Rather than people

Land it woke and entailed answers

They recruited legs and other features

It had been an owl's nest now without the owl

Touch lifted the avenue very high

Some mastery of the wind meant years of revenge

Tell the end before arrivals

That stretch meant delinquency in how

Qualities of tenor and harp on delays

Forget the answer, not knowing it ever

Rain delays, mind delays, asking where

Wishlist remainder, who of the nest

Wisdom cut into intelligence

Fraught allies to see

Memorialize a quench

Topically aligned

Break through: glass ceiling veneer, hostility

Land in the gully with glasses

April 22, 2019

Same same same and we knew

The strategies reviled quickly

Fiercely contained deliberate gesture

Frontally destined silver forlorn

Long term nudging and amendment

Forty-two aspects of heroism

Debt ration storing inward

Change remind to detach

Tell quark and removal ration

Forty-seven calculus of landing

Cannily remains if turmeric

Cat call and wishes float

Fraught tumble of bedrock

Sixth sense to the dragonfly rush

December 4, 2019

The remainder of the cast fell off the stage

We were swaying in circles of dilemmas

Some misty intention had deranged the mares

Quickly in a frosty sea the talent of angels

Others quieted and untangled

The land stacked on land stacked on land

Such furry acceptance of fuel through the veins

In a commentary mellow and triad, fully wished

A container of penniless substance soaked in gas

Further cues how to live while dying

Cement in the veins (she said she said) the cat

Fruitfully lest the vacuum pump freeze

You see she knew, she knew the rain fell vociferously

The things you say along an island dismissal

A faculty of letters slip down the stairs

Scrape on the backs of knees

It was this and again this

(it had been screaming at you all this time)

Missions in figs and long dismissals

However the rotten remainder told the island

Because no one can hear till their eardrums nearly break

Further cues of plates, forks, cucumbers & stocks

Each would be sliced down the middle

Until a meaning derived

An entry into the epitome of ether

Determined by quantities of lead and eggs and underwear

A quotient factory please into dismissal

How laughing they admired the sun set that way

To foreclose the erasure of a temple along

December 5

It was mellow and it was tainted, severally this year

Others required expectancy a frozen time

17 times, was it? the ETC

you could try to be by her side, just like by the incubator

But nothing you can do so often

Things are happening

On city streets hundreds of people going the other way

Qualitative forensic medicine

But what was it you meant

And you watching Grand Central Station

Thinking of Robin Williams' vision: all dancing

Fruitfully positioned along a river

The building cascading

All their material faces into sadness

Relations soft and deniable formidable

Landlocked inquisitive futuricity

The presidencies all the same, sort of

A potato in the earth—this is life?

How can we deny the light

And if you landed there some minutes

A lock of oil: addicted to hating it

Then the letting go of a covered moss

Forfeit control along the delay

Soul food she said there were pockets

The correspondence formally of between cats

Then another howling of souls

Quick entities and coral reefs

All that is there and how it coexists

A fleeting impression because of that cloud

What was you wanted in that speck?

How could you align it so plainly

A former claim of dialing it in

Useful probation has an hour

In a zippy conundrum of laugh

December 6

A box of rainbows just unfurled on the train tracks

Glinting cabin fever quickly calls

A thousand stakes of cranberry along melt

We touch barely or quickly the zany

Far along a measure of zest the quick way

Terribly filtered and familiar quest zone

A characteristic of hollow down throughout

Forsaken and mellow now the tides

A transient fever first inhibited by lines

Quaking and sarcastic frivolous demeanor

Fortuitous the stack of plates toward this

Possible how's tossed and cowering forthwith

Mesmerize crescendos of a certain talent

Fierce delays to a cloud caught under its own rain

West of the apple a surging of degrees

A quaking mingling of hourglass stupor

Vying for the lane of quirky entanglement

As best we can in the pavement: all the way through

A zealous dismissal of the fourth branch

Quizzically demanding lands of attention

How do we lane and say it to the making

Subside undertones of substantial watching

How the spoon turned back at the park

More zealously caught in the snow and fire

Landing directly waking indiscriminately

Attest to markings of quicksand

The connection between bikes and flames and pensions

A marginal causality how to tender

It was you and it was you whether to how

Calling the geese cats formally milk rangers

Trusted among aspects of nurture

Foresworn truces and dimensions forthcoming

December 8

Can you regurgitate an arrow

You thought the answer was no

Further sales qualitatively determined by freight

Can you command an independent frost

Generally the answer is no to the power of yes

Maimed by a mystery of telling

He said the literature may rise to the occasion

Some doctrine queried anger

Forcefully dimensional and discrete

You too, you, too the hour is upon you

Can the arrangement slip through possibility

Lengthen the defeat to stretcher

More to the point, docks in attention: out there

The solemn reminder to dress and feature

A silly solution quakes in the dressing

Four more piles of focus to the slip

Lanes late into the missive quick time

Mainly horrendous and challenging

Out of pace with the splendor

Dying along a ladder of community

Longing to retreat into a cloud which turns into a whale

So to mellow resolutions zany and torn

Quick quick quick slow down

Where is the manual and the addendum

How to plant laughter in a bed of oil

You wished for the trick or solution

Replies replies What is the solution

The corporate silence has no soul

What are we thinking, undo, undo

What would I give to have an egg

Rather than google appear in my hand

December 10

How many decibels into the rain?

Rain not rain quickening the synapses

Further along and solemn chatter

Honor the alarm into the seriousness of the call

How the animals fell (we must hold them now)

The angle of shock depleting attention

Volumes supplemented by their cacophony

December 11

Quickly woman decided into throttling ease & betrayal

Formerly couched mockingly so along lanes into rapture

Insistently in a quandary forever tipped in mud

The lane of assault determined it fashion

And the passing branches whisk into fields

Must it be so, what color are you?

We are equal inside says the six-year-old

Frolicking truth, let it be so, how to say?

Remainders of truth and synonymous heroes

Frankly the alignment taking you singularly

A froth of running wolves to the tale

Merely something synonymous under the waking sky

You surely, you GET IT, don't you?

There was a coffee for you & some cigarettes

Veinly defying our desire to defend and measure

How do you underscore its engines

Markedly out the door in the breezed

There were eggs, and He, he was a good one

Showers and pinnacles of precipitation

It was all we wanted to know

Cheese and other rinds of feeling, must tell

Adamantly defying the thought recitation

A mix of completion and lefthanded song

A house of mustering of left attention

How to arrange the telling of the quandary

Mixing and denying the quaint muster

A tenacity of approach to a toxic degree

Never was it possible further entrenched

More or less raining on the leftover attention

But I said that before: a frolicking departure

Some truffle tenses quickly signed off and patted down

How to determine or allay the certain death?

There we were going along (there's nothing alone I can do)

How to retreat even further into address?

It was the cat's ear, she said, she said

You are one person who is doing something. There is you.

You move mountains and streams

You move, you move mountains and streams

You move, you move places and people, ground

For if we angle along gently the hills

How to touch it or inquire: who to ask

What the scale of the annunciation along imagining

It all of a sudden came back to us

The marked attention of it all, simultaneously

How to determine who will be entering

And what satisfies the nerve of some drops

Landing to the measure of quickness

Who she said and ran, so they knew

Defeat, a rail, and the two robins

The last attachment was you in there

December 12

How was it the rain set your hair down

For to the wish of aim long to the zoom

More we watched more it delivered

Pastry and formula down catching mellow

Formerly and latterly who fell to the attributed

Mired in attention quasi held

Fortuitous how that mess quaked up

And they angled it wishing more in a mellow filter

Zones of breath, a quirky dilemma

Questions of saying the frozen tasting a humility

There in the perturbance of emotion running back

A tossed remainder filling the station

We were quirky and certain

Full-flung attention wishing similitude

Makeshift alarms unto petrol

A question frightening frosty demeanor

Letting out along me to the taking

December 17

Forsworn and melodic, happily dependent on endings

A zany reply to the forcing of the cattle

Many remainders of the last thought

How you diminished your hours in this

A quick kind of thinking: it was your mama

Frightfully she approached and it became intuitive

Such devotion solidifying before your eyes

Where the souls—wrapped around the old telephone poles

A search for mixing tenures thoroughly portrayed

Furnished to a wintering apple (bite, bite)

The sick sense of things, and of them

A crown across the thickness of demand

A quarry of soldiers pecking around impeachment

Me it was me who would lose in the end

We favored the qualities of melting snow

Whether it was left or right, I counted

And yet we are human, can't get beyond that

Shaking the remainders of ourselves into some shape

Melodies to the right, to the left

Whereas in no particular direction

Landing at this alley in an asymptote

Dimensions of non-being further to claim it

Like some kind of bag tag warped and wended

We were gone astray, had been linked together

Features of that wisdom, bits of starlight entered through

Quickly diminished and outlaid, the studies on grass

Left to tell you, thoroughly or not, what find

Who was it who laid into, among the straw

Could we wish you a patent or a mystery

Linking us together at day's end

Further like a crushing red stone

Hollow, hollow to the back of it, some say

A virtual roller coaster of iron retreats

Sickness into mellow what quietude of avenue

December 23

How to dawdle and demand at one time

The quizzical look of oppression further inward

A wish for rigor and syllables granted

Applied along scenarios these ones

And you hop through the interstices in a flurry of compassion

Multiple fruits of labors and value

A designed avenue into intuition

A way of navigating and saying yes

A reign too of retreats and demands

How was the wash enough thinking through the division

The sick custom of the eleventh hour

Mortally cursed into a reindeer of change

Say the vanilla tossing of the bridge

A mellow kiss savoring rain and shallow

A merit of stagnation frequently arraigned

More to the temper of arraignment

Following the catch of slim fellows

January 20, 2020

The less thoughtful compatriot ran thoroughly through

Frankly hackled and demanded

Sullenly queried and trebled

Mystified, quickened, arranged

What's this the thickness of delay

Wrestled away from matter

February 5, 2020

A kindred spirit delayed our gratification

Mellow and tumultuous said how

A friction of remaining cows

How to generate the thoughts

Culinary and demanding

Some solemn reminders of mortality

Freshly caught dimensions rendered solid

Here is the Rabbit whose ears can't hear

Says Joy

February 27

The children were all in maps and rows

We held in our hands possibility in all colors

The sense of it was a journey into turquoise

Remainders of excess in a time of should-be rationing

The call of intent determined the energy

Some shock in the juncture surely as an eye

For tomorrow is another day we had not planned for

Today so insistent, so many demands

With its quirky timing, a hand in the mirror

Functioning alert or caught within an engine

Some other mounds of detection

See this little inch of freedom in which you sleep

(they want that)

The imagination is universal, in turtles

They have survived the dinosaurs, here with us in shells

March 2020

It was the continuance of tomorrow and it was today

The threatened species could not see the threatening ones

Only water and wind

The remainder of the hour was a lane of thought

Suddenly tracking the last of the light

We could pretend to divide and congregate

April 25, 2020

It is the who what when time

It is the how time the if time

It is the wren time the itch time

The crescendo of magic time

Saying to a following of heart time

Some wings and other promising land time

Solely connected in that concavity

The little ring of a cat time

The hollowed ooh time

The watch pot tea time

The southwestnortheastardly wind time

Author's Note

When I began this book, I was thinking of Lyn Hejinian's *My Life* (1980), and the frame of the number. In the first edition of that book, Lyn wrote 37 sections with 37 sentences each, in conjunction with her age at the time. I was drawn to the courage of the form, the decision to stay in the moment, to let language follow the pace of the mind.

I was 47 when I began, going to the same café, with an urge to write 47 discrete sentences in 47 minutes each time. I felt no need to have coherence from line to line, but instead tried to let each line be its own thing and then start again. I love to make a decision for a poetry book or series about what it needs to be, and then do it, even if I fall short, break the form, twist the goal, as I did here.

Before writing these poems, I had spent a lot of time with Bernadette Mayer's *Memory* (1971) when it appeared as a show in Manhattan in 2017. In that series, Mayer kept a journal and shot a roll of 35mm film daily. I was thinking about the notion of a series—of life and consciousness happening in the moment, and being in the speed of it, without judging or forming conclusions, just staying with its language and mental visuals. I felt as though this would make possible a kind of cinema verité of the subconscious through poetic association and its momentum. A book, I thought, could be a cinema of language, in the flow of language that accompanies the mind, in associative movement.

Though I was writing in the midst of a Trump presidency, of national reckonings, and of family crises, I thought these poems could act as a sequence of reels and separated frames that are only abstractly about "my life."

I see this book as part of a series that mixes "technologies of communication." When I was writing my dissertation on the impact of visual technologies—cinema, postcards, and optics—on mid-century American poetry (later published as *Word Sightings*), an advisor said: "You know, writing is also a technology."

Lines are a technology as well as a category, a shape, a way of making meaning. I was doing a series of paintings prior and simultaneous to this book, just of lines. Vertical rather than horizontal. The atmosphere was dire and I could not read the news. Instead I changed directions.

At one point in *Lines*, language breaks down, becomes incoherent nonsense—a kind of language collapse. And yet, even in nonsense, there are patterns, meaning, a kind of beauty to be found in the madness—snapshots of uncomfortable confrontations and toxic situations, as well as utopian possibilities.

In the end, this book reaches for the underbelly of language—the undercurrents—what isn't said. May it send out ripples to all those with underspoken thought processes to release and circulate.

Acknowledgments

I am grateful to early readers of this manuscript, including Susan Gevirtz, Peter Gizzi, Ghazal Mosadeq, Jérémy Robert, and J. Mae Barizo and the writing group we were in together. Thank you, Erik King for your close read and editorial suggestions. Thanks to Ed Bowes, Susan Gevirtz, and Malvika Jolly for feedback on the afterword. Thanks also to Tasnim Ara and the OS Café for providing a place to work.

An earlier version of a section of this book appeared in the anthology *Queenzsenglish*, edited by Kyoo Lee with help from James Sherry. Poems from the book have also appeared in *Annulet*, *The Chalamet Review*, *Hurricane Review*, *Jacket2*, and *VOLT*. My gratitude to the editors.

Deep appreciation for writing sessions with Safaa Fathy and Tracy Grinnell in which I edited some of these poems, and to Anne Waldman for guiding word choice and tone across my work of recent years.

Special thanks to stellar editor and publisher Matvei Yankelevich of Winter Editions for tremendous involvement and outreach for this book.

Thanks to Gia Hamilton for being there, and to Omar Berrada and our families for their enduring support.

SARAH RIGGS is a poet and artist based in Brooklyn. She received the 1913 Poetry Prize for her book *Pomme & Granite* and her translation of Etel Adnan's *Time* won the Griffin International Prize and Best Translated Book Award. *Word Sightings*, her essays on the impact of visual media on US poetry, was published by Routledge. With her partner Omar Berrada, Riggs runs Tamaas, an intercultural arts organization focusing on translation, film and education, and co-edited *Another Room to Live In: 15 Contemporary Arab Poets* (Litmus). Written during the 2016–2020 Trump presidency, along with *The Nerve Epistle* (Roof), *Lines* is her eighth book of poems.

Lines
Copyright © Sarah Riggs, 2025

ISBN 978-1-959708-12-4
LCCN 2025930680

First Edition, 2025 — 1,000 copies

Winter Editions, Brooklyn, New York
wintereditions.net

The cover features a detail of an artwork by Sara Ouhaddou: "Study for *Igdad* [The Birds]," ink on paper, 2016. Printed with permission of the artist.

WE books are typeset in Heldane, a renaissance-inspired serif designed by Kris Sowersby for Klim Type Foundry, and Zirkon, a contemporary gothic designed by Tobias Rechsteiner for Grilli Type. The layout and covers are done by the editor following a series design by Andrew Bourne.

This book was printed and bound in Lithuania by BALTO print with eco-friendly Munken papers. Manufactured by Arctic Paper in Sweden, Munken meets EU Ecolabel, Forest Stewardship Council, and Cradle to Cradle certification standards.

WE is grateful for the support of our subscribers, and extends special thanks to recent Supporting and Lifetime Subscribers: Anonymous, Anonymous (in memory of the Beaubiens), Yevgeniy Fiks, Elizabeth T. Gray, Jr., and Katy Lederer.

WE is a member of the Community of Literary Magazines and Presses (CLMP). Our 2025 program is supported by a Small Press Future Fund grant from CLMP and the Mellon Foundation.

 Winter Editions

Emily Simon, IN MANY WAYS

Garth Graeper, THE SKY BROKE MORE

Robert Desnos, NIGHT OF LOVELESS NIGHTS, tr. Lewis Warsh

Richard Hell, WHAT JUST HAPPENED

Marina Tëmkina & Michel Gérard, BOYS FIGHT

Claire DeVoogd, VIA

Monica McClure, THE GONE THING

Ahmad Almallah, BORDER WISDOM

Hélio Oiticica, SECRET POETICS, tr. Rebecca Kosick

Heimrad Bäcker, DOCUMENTARY POETRY, tr. Patrick Greaney

Robert Fitterman, CREVE COEUR

Karla Kelsey, TRANSCENDENTAL FACTORY: FOR MINA LOY

Alan Gilbert, THE EVERYDAY LIFE OF DESIGN

Betsy Fagin, FIRES SEEN FROM SPACE

Cristina Pérez Díaz, FROM THE FOUNDING OF THE COUNTRY

Sarah Riggs, LINES

Leah Flax Barber, THE MIRROR OF SIMPLE SOULS

Michael Kasper, START ANYWHERE

POSTCARDS OF THE SIEGE: VISUAL CULTURE DURING THE SIEGE OF LENINGRAD (1941–1944), ed. Polina Barskova

Nathalie Quintane, THE CAVALIER, tr. Jonathan Larson

Monique Wittig, THE LESBIAN BODY, tr. David LeVay

Monique Wittig, ACROSS THE ACHERON, tr. David LeVay